The Know It All Book of Oenology

Waldo Rochow, MBA

Published by the author
Edited by Will Rochow
Cover by Waldo Rochow
    with elements of *The portal* by: pualv (www.flickr.com/photos/8460740@N05)
    CC-BY 2.0 (accessed: 27 Jul 2014)

Website: http:// know-it-all.rochow.info

ISBN: 978-0-9938818-9-3

Any resemblance to persons living or dead is purely coincidental. This is
original work conceived by the author; any perception of plagiarism is
also purely coincidental.

Volume #23 in the ***Know It All*** series:

The Know It All Book of Astronomy	*The Know It All Book of Leadership*
The Know It All Book of Biology	*The Know It All Book of Literature*
The Know It All Book of Business	*The Know It All Book of Marketing*
The Know It All Book of Chemistry	*The Know It All Book of Mathematics*
The Know It All Book of Climate Change	*The Know It All Book of Meteorology*
The Know It All Book of Conservation	*The Know It All Book of Music*
The Know It All Book of Economics	*The Know It All Book of Oceanography*
The Know It All Book of Education	*The Know It All Book of Oenology*
The Know It All Book of Equality	*The Know It All Book of Peace*
The Know It All Book of Gastronomy	*The Know It All Book of Physics*
The Know It All Book of Geology	*The Know It All Book of Politics*
The Know It All Book of Geopolitics	*The Know It All Book of Poverty*
The Know It All Book of Health Care	*The Know It All Book of Psychiatry*
The Know It All Book of History	*The Know It All Book of Technology*
The Know It All Book of Justice	*The Know It All Book of Theology*

To my loving wife Joanne, for putting up
with my silly side all these years;

To my sons Karl and Paul, for following in
my silly shoes;

To my parents, for instilling in all your kids
and grandkids an appreciation for the silly
side of life;

To my brother Will, for your tireless editing
support; and

To all the people of the world, for giving me
something to laugh about.

Thank you for joining me on this journey. The purpose of this book is actually deeper than its tongue-in-cheek treatment here suggests. While on the surface it might appear that I am scoffing at higher learning, nothing could be further from the truth. It is my goal to encourage the reader to think, and study, and to not be satisfied with the status quo. In fact, I would be thrilled if you fill this book with your own observations.

As someone with an interest in this subject, why shouldn't you write *The Book of Knowledge*? You just might be seen by future generations as the *Father* or *Mother* of the study of Oenology. Sure, you won't be the first author on the subject (after all, neither was I), but you could be the most significant.

I hope that you will become a contagion of inquisitiveness. Be that gal or that guy that is constantly asking *why*. Contaminate your friends and family with curiosity. Consider the possibility that much, if not all, that we know today on any subject may be completely wrong. Challenge the assumptions upon which your knowledge is based.

You just might be surprised what you can still learn after you
know it all.

-- Waldo Rochow, MBA

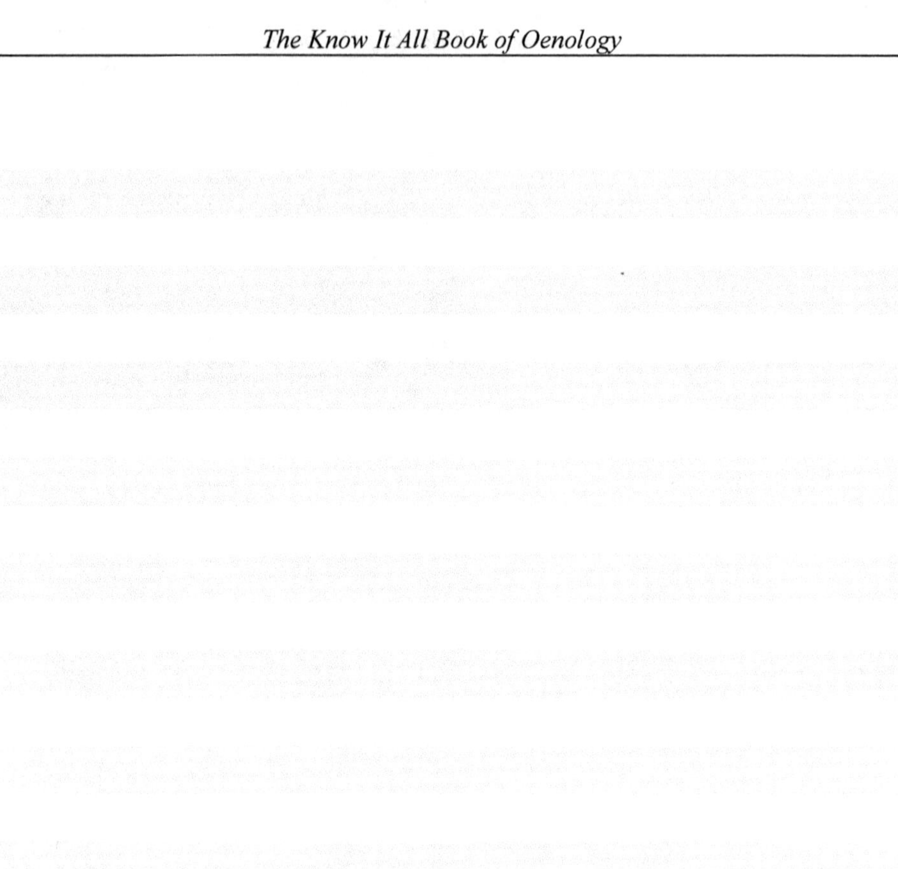

www.ingramcontent.com/pod-product-compliance
Lightning Source LLC
Chambersburg PA
CBHW070956040426
42443CB00007B/538